A GUIDE TO SILCHESTER

THE ROMAN TOWN OF CALLEVA ATREBATUM

Michael Fulford

NEW EDITION
2002

INTRODUCTION

The Iron Age and Roman settlement of Calleva Atrebatum lies in the north of Hampshire in the parish of Silchester, roughly midway between the modern towns of Basingstoke and Reading.

The site is remarkable because, unlike most large Roman towns in Britain, it was completely abandoned. The defensive walls still survive, in places more than 4m high, but within the walls there seems, at first, to be nothing but fields, a church and a single house, once a farm.

The town was built on an easily defensible spur of gravel about 90m above sea level, with commanding views to the east and south and the only access over level ground from the west.

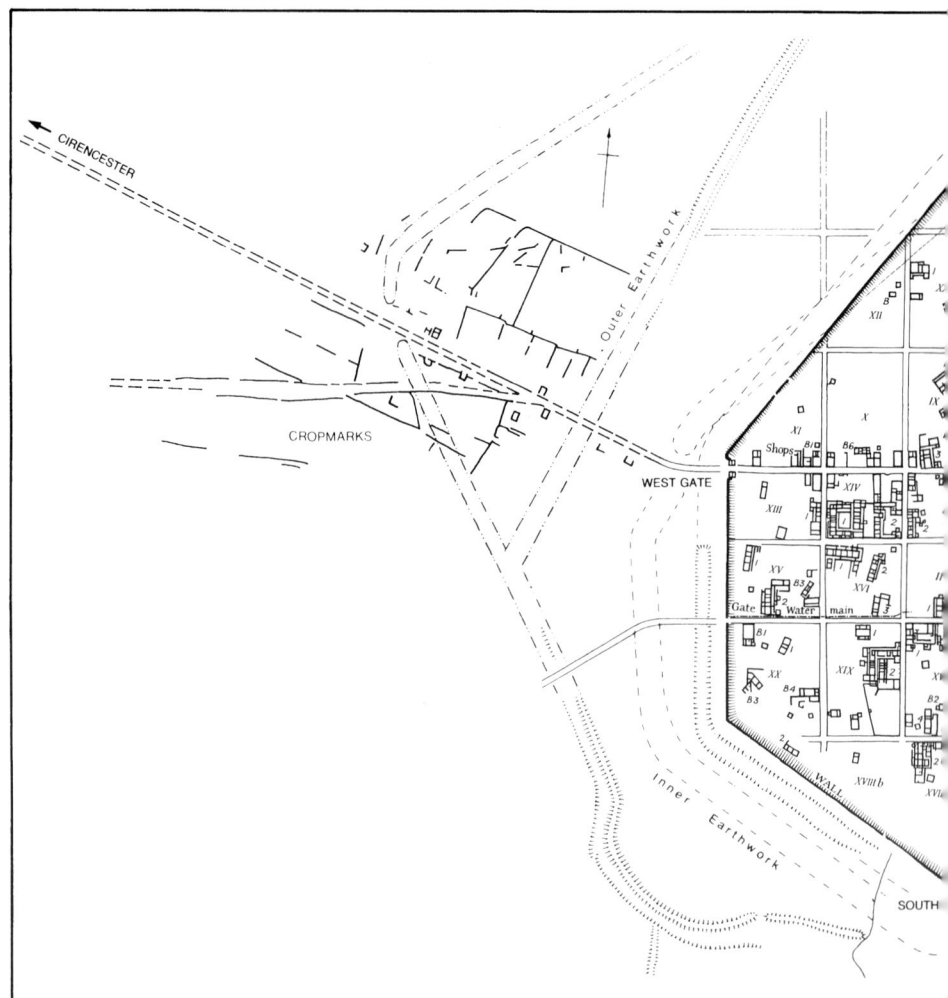

INTRODUCTION

It was originally surrounded on three sides by woodland, growing on the heavy clay soils, and this aspect of the site is enshrined within the Celtic name, which can be translated as (the town in the) woods of the Atrebates.

While the surrounding woodland provided fuel and building materials and hindered easy access to the settlement, the gravel spur itself was more easily cleared for cultivation and building by the first occupants. As the numerous wells on the site demonstrate, water was abundant from about 3-4m below ground surface and from springs around the edge of the gravel.

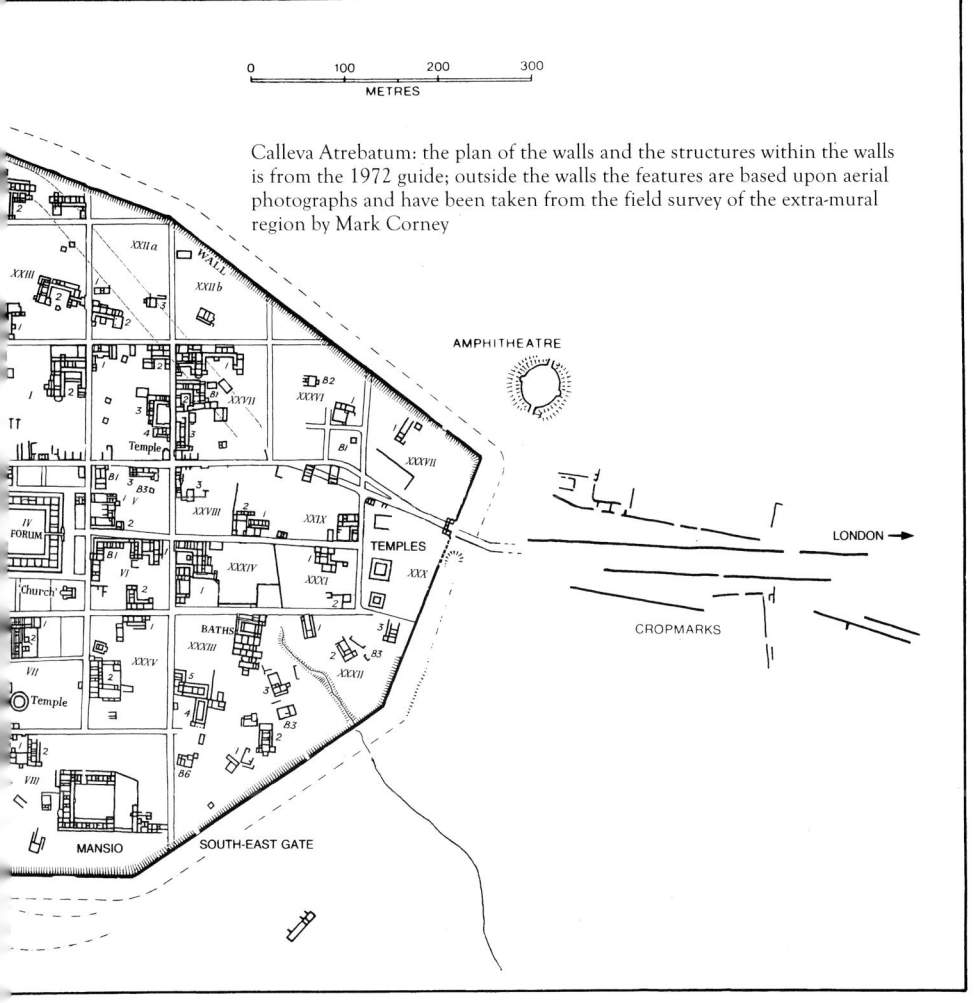

Calleva Atrebatum: the plan of the walls and the structures within the walls is from the 1972 guide; outside the walls the features are based upon aerial photographs and have been taken from the field survey of the extra-mural region by Mark Corney

PRE-ROMAN CALLEVA

The most impressive remains of the Iron Age period are the earthworks to the west of the Roman town wall. Along part of the section to the southwest, in Rampier Copse, the crest still rises almost 5m above the ditch. Within these earthworks, in the area of the later basilica, excavations have revealed evidence of dense occupation from about 25BC.

A mass of material, both artefactual and environmental, reveals a very Romanised population with evidence in the form of styli and graffiti for writing in Latin. Quantities of pottery were imported from northern and central France as well as the Mediterranean regions, including containers for wine, olive oil and other preserved foods. Oysters, otherwise unknown from inland Iron Age sites, were abundant and the presence of fowl and the proportion of pork and beef to other meats are also indicative of habits quite different from those of the local population in the countryside. Even in the choice of building materials, we see a preference for oak, a wood generally favoured by Roman carpenters.

By the beginning of the first century AD remains of streets at right angles to each other indicate the possibility of

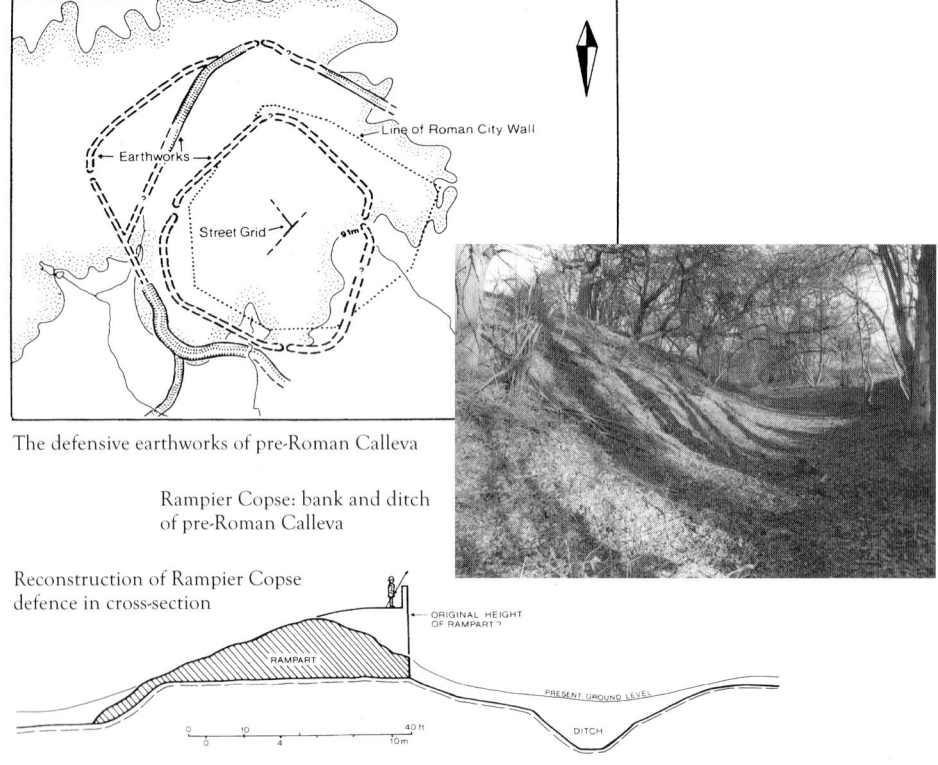

The defensive earthworks of pre-Roman Calleva

Rampier Copse: bank and ditch of pre-Roman Calleva

Reconstruction of Rampier Copse defence in cross-section

PRE-ROMAN CALLEVA

some regular planning made up of rectangular plots and timber-framed buildings. If this layout proves to encompass the whole Iron Age settlement, it will give the appearance of a Roman town with its regular street grid and town blocks (*insulae*). Protected at the same time by a new defensive rampart (the inner earthwork) the settlement covered some 32ha (80 acres) and continued to develop in this form up to the mid-to-late first century AD.

Iron Age round houses on the basilica site, with, below, a reconstruction of a round house under constrcution

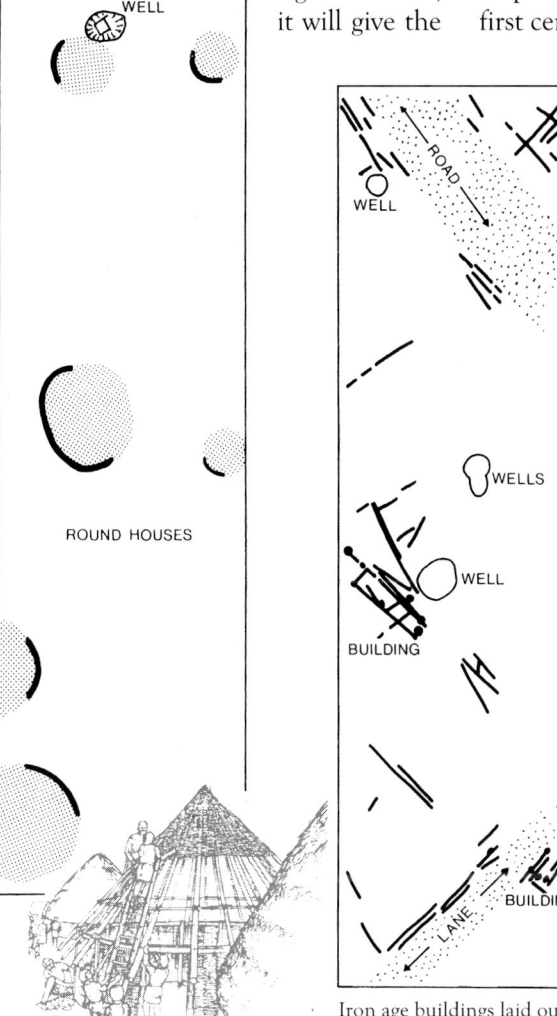

Iron age buildings laid out on a rectangular grid in the late first century B.C.

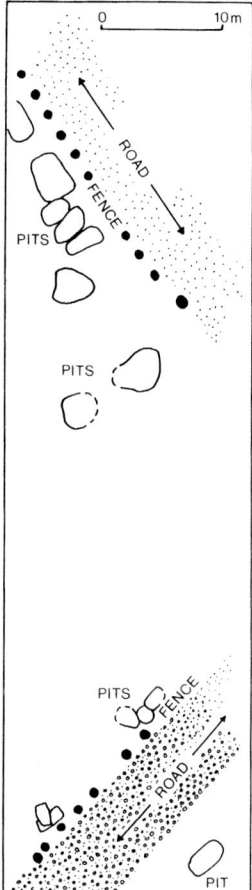

Street grid with flanking fences and pits from the latest Iron Age phase in the early first century A.D.

KINGS OF THE ATREBATES

To the pre-Roman period we can attribute the coins of Eppillus, self-styled REX (king), which carry the marks of CALLE or CALLEV and are generally regarded as having been produced at Calleva. Eppillus described himself as son of Commius, a claim he shared with two other leaders, Tincomarus and Verica. While Tincomarus, fleeing to Rome by AD 7, was probably ousted by Eppillus, Eppillus himself appears to have been ejected by his brother Verica who ruled until the beginning of the 40s, when he was forced out of Britain, probably by the Catuvellaunian prince, Epatticus or Caratacus. It is reasonable to presume that all three ruled from Silchester for some or all of their respective reigns. The fact that they all claimed to be descendants of a certain Commius, who is usually identified as the Gallic leader of the Atrebates who escaped to

Gold coin of Eppillus inscribed CALLEV (Calleva) reproduced twice actual size

Gold stater of Commius twice actual size

Reconstruction of an Iron Age war chariot

KINGS OF THE ATREBATES

Gold stater of Tincomarus

twice actual size

Britain from Julius Caesar about 50 BC, adds weight to the hypothesis that Commius was the original founder of Calleva.

What role did pre-Roman Calleva play? Following the description furnished by the Greek geographer Strabo, writing in the late first century BC about exports from Britain as a whole, we may envisage Calleva as drawing tribute in the form of corn, cattle, hides, slaves and other raw materials from the Atrebatic territory of central southern Britain as well as trading for similar commodities from more distant parts of Britain. These goods were exchanged for cash, luxury food-stuffs and manufactured items from the Roman world.

There is certainly evidence for the production of a range of bronze metalwork, principally horse-gear, and, as signalled above, a strong probability of the minting of coinage in precious metals. Such trade seems also to have passed through the hands of other groups, such as the Catuvellauni, immediate neighbours to the east of Calleva. As the expanded distribution of their coins indicates, a desire for further control may have been one of the reasons behind the Catuvellaunian occupation of Atrebatic territory, including Calleva, in the years immediately preceding the Roman invasion.

Silver minim of Verica (above)
Coins twice actual size
Gold stater of Verica (right)

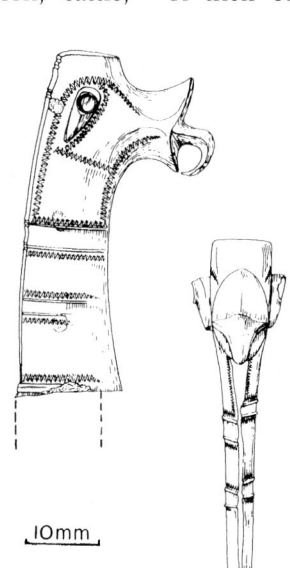

10mm

Late Iron Age bronze razor-handle

CALLEVA AND THE CLIENT KINGDOM OF COGIDUBNUS

The plan yielded by the Victorian and Edwardian excavations is, very largely, that of the walled town in the later third and fourth centuries. Like its early Iron Age predecessor, the early Roman town of the first and second centuries is largely unknown.

It is reasonable to associate Calleva with the client kingdom of Cogidubnus right from the start. One of the reasons given for the Roman invasion of Britain in AD 43 was to assist a certain Berikos, who is usually identified with Verica, whose kingdom at one time had included Calleva. Whether Verica was restored in AD 43 or the kingdom was established at the outset in the name of Cogidubnus, it is likely that Calleva formed part of it. In the context of an independent kingdom, it is probable, considering Calleva's size and status, that a Roman garrison was stationed here, if only briefly, in the 40s, but no certain evidence of it has yet been found. To this period belongs a major timber building of Roman style erected

Conjectured plan of the first forum, showing the excavated features of the west range. The later Basilica-Forum is show in dotted outline.

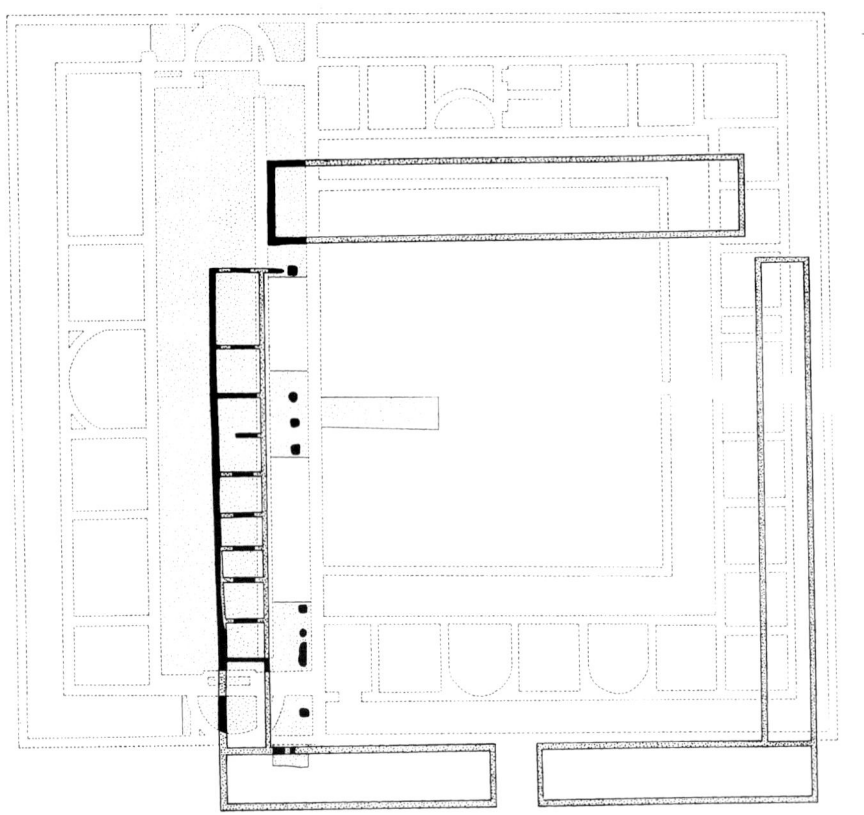

CALLEVA AND THE CLIENT KINGDOM OF COGIDUBNUS

on the site of the later forum basilica in the centre of the town.

Traces of the early town can be glimpsed in all those buildings which do not conform to the later Roman street grid, and which can be discerned over most of the area within the later walls and beyond. Among the more notable are the public baths, the amphitheatre and at least three temples. The discovery of bricks stamped with the abbreviated name of the emperor Nero (AD 54-68) suggests official involvement in this early development of the town.

Neronian tile-stamp reading NER(O) CL(AUDIUS) CAE(SAR) AUG(USTUS) GER(MANICUS)

Purbeck marble inscription naming the town (CALLEVAE) in the penultimate line

Translation: ... without their contributions gave from his (or their) own resources this gift entrusted to him (or them) by the guild of *peregrini* at *Calleva*

ROMAN CALLEVA

Since there is no coherent plan in the orientation of the buildings assigned to the Calleva of the client kingdom, it is not surprising that a major re-planning of the town took place in the later first century with the laying down of a regular grid of streets which shaped the development of the town thereafter. The blocks (*insulae*) are remarkably consistent in their dimensions, approximately 400 by 400 or 275 by 400 Roman feet. Central to the central block is the forum basilica, a mixture of market and administrative centre, which was first constructed in timber about 85.

This building symbolically marks the transition from the town of the client kingdom to that of the administrative centre of the civitas of the Atrebates. The tribal area represents a fraction of that of the earlier kingdom extending only across the modern counties of Berkshire, north Hampshire, south Oxfordshire and into Surrey and Wiltshire to east and west respectively. Calleva's responsibility was to dispense justice based on tribal law and to raise imperial and local taxes. The town probably also served as the most important market of the region, as the prominent

The Flavian Forum-Basilica of about AD 85, showing the excavated features and the conjectured plan of the rest of the Forum The later Forum and Basilica are shown in dotted outline

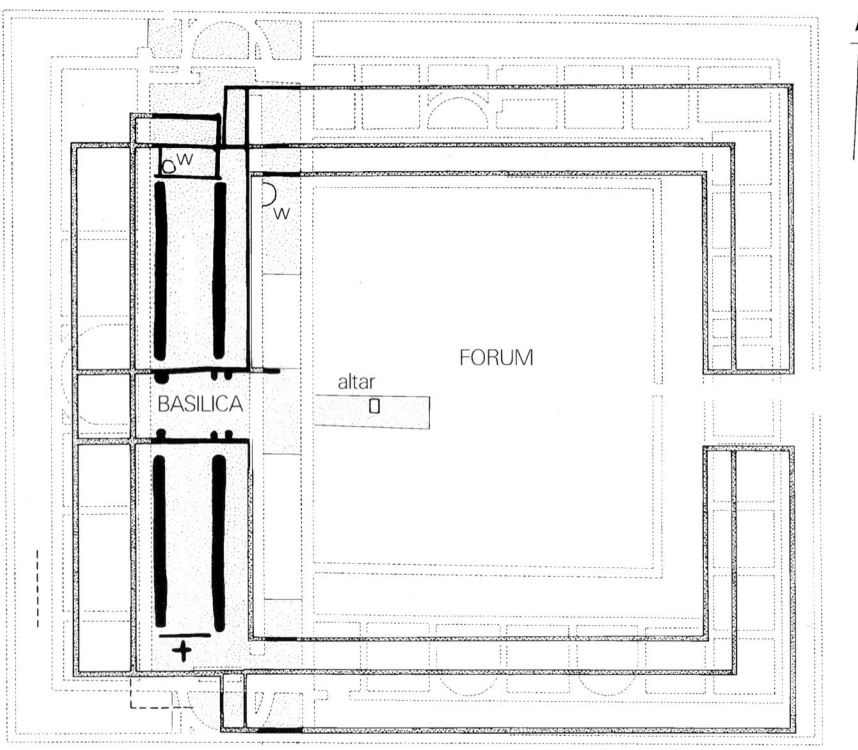

ROMAN CALLEVA

building (*forum*) and the range of narrow-fronted shop-units along the main east-west street and elsewhere proclaim. It was on these activities, as well as the income from estates outside the town, that the population depended throughout the Roman period.

There is no certain evidence available to suggest that Calleva Atrebatum ever attained the status of a municipium or chartered town, where the citizens had voting rights, but this may have been granted as early as the time of the creation of the civitas. It is difficult to estimate the population of the town, but if suburbs are excluded and calculations confined to the known buildings within the Roman defences, a minimum figure of about 1200 is reached. Without written evidence there can be neither certainty about numbers, nor how they fluctuated with time, but we should remember that figures as high as 7500 and as low as 600-750 have also been estimated.

Like most of the towns of Roman Britain Calleva prospered without defences until the end of the second century when it was provided with a rampart of gravel and clay into which were set masonry gates. This circuit enclosed about 43 ha (107 acres) and was replaced in stone in the later third century, about 260-80. Despite the existence of the wall, life in the suburbs continued to flourish until the late fourth century.

Probable Roman administrative territory (*civitas*) of the Atrebates

Reconstruction of the shops on the main road leading to the west gate

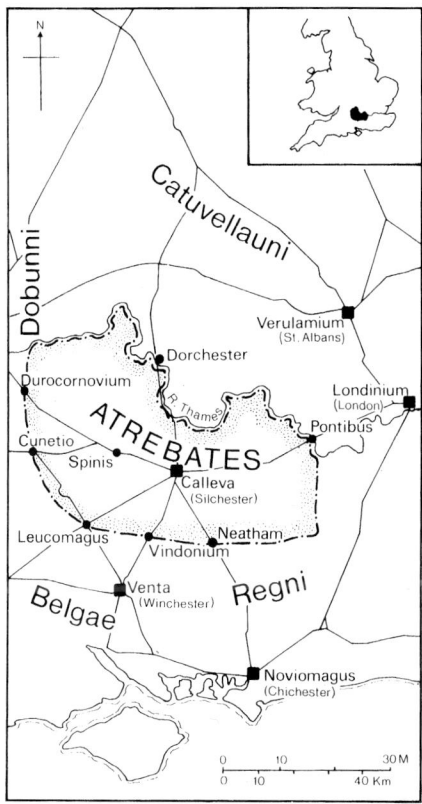

THE AMPHITHEATRE

The amphitheatre was probably first built between about AD 50 and 70 at the eastern edge of the town. The arena now has an elliptical plan with two opposing entrances on the longer, north-south axis and two small rooms recessed into the seating bank on the east-west axis. It measures about 45 by 39 metres.

Soil from the area of the arena, whose surface lies some 2 metres below the original ground level, was used to build up the seating banks. At first the inner faces of the banks were retained by an almost circular timber revetment, a wall which may have had the additional function of supporting timber terracing for spectators.

In the third century, after modifications and periods of disuse, the arena was refurbished and the timber revetment was replaced by a wall of flint and brown ironstone, the lower courses of which remain. Originally about 3 metres high it also served to support seating arrangements which continued to be of wood. On the east and west sides are semi-circular niches which were prob-

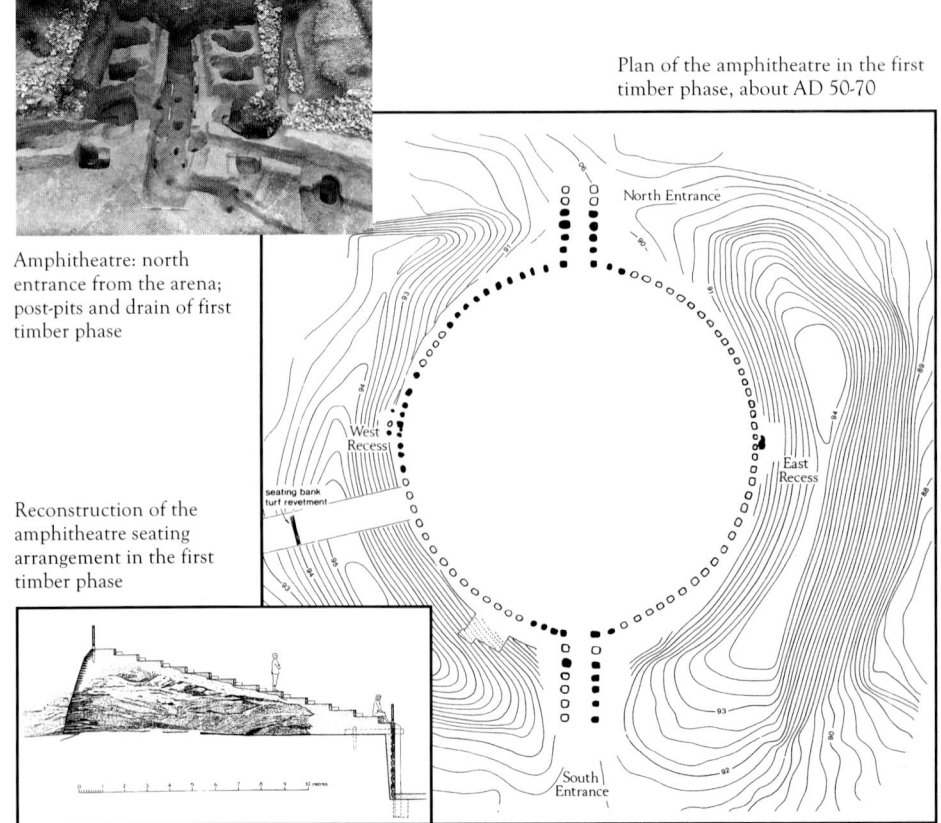

Amphitheatre: north entrance from the arena; post-pits and drain of first timber phase

Reconstruction of the amphitheatre seating arrangement in the first timber phase

Plan of the amphitheatre in the first timber phase, about AD 50-70

THE AMPHITHEATRE

ably once vaulted. There is no evidence as to how they were used, but similar recesses elsewhere have contained altars to Nemesis (fate). Alternatively, they may have served as refuges for participants in the games held in the arena.

The banks of the seats in the amphitheatre provided space for between 4,500 and 9,000 spectators. No evidence survives of the sort of activities which took place here, but gladiatorial combat and shows using wild beasts were popular, but expensive, forms of entertainment elsewhere in the Roman empire. Blood sports using bulls, dogs and bears are possibilities at Silchester. Public executions also took place in amphitheatres.

These monuments have to be distinguished from theatres, the traditional venue for dramatic entertainment. No theatre has yet been discovered at Calleva.

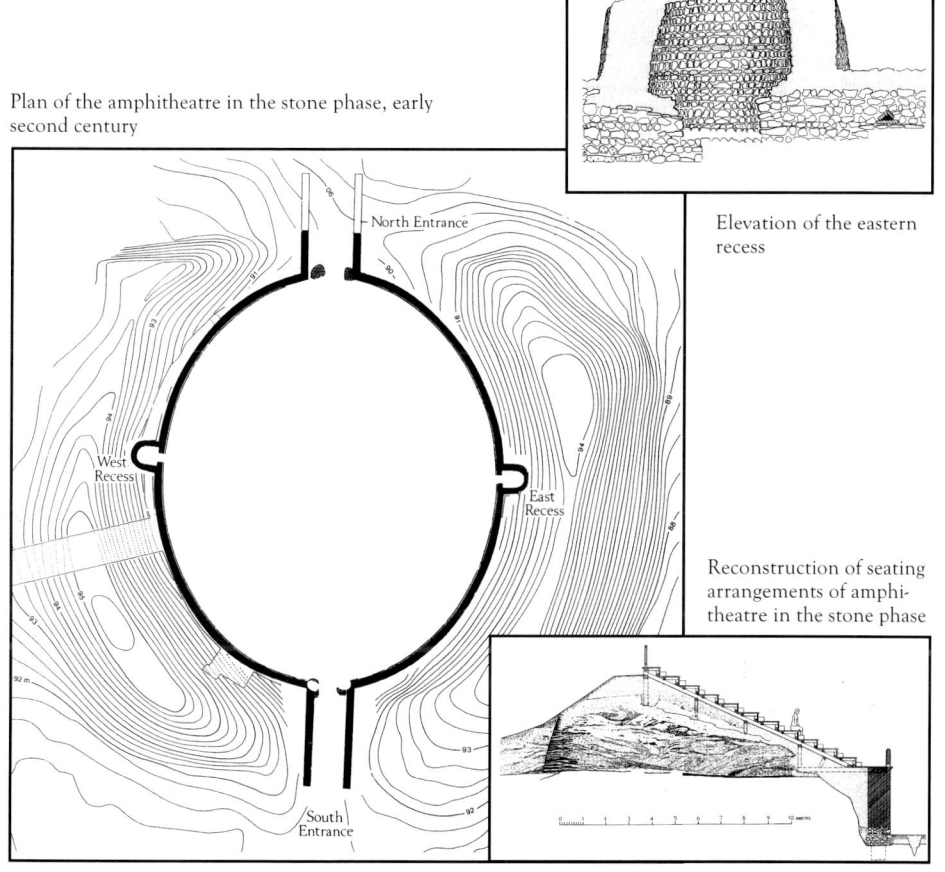

Plan of the amphitheatre in the stone phase, early second century

Elevation of the eastern recess

Reconstruction of seating arrangements of amphitheatre in the stone phase

THE DEFENCES

Watercolour of the South Gate from the notebook of Rev. J. Joyce, 1872 (right)

Reconstruction of the west gate (below)

There is no certain evidence that the town was provided with any form of protection until the very end of the second century. At this time, in common with many other towns, Calleva was provided with a single rampart of clay and gravel derived from two V-shaped ditches in front of it. Accompanying this simple form of defence were much more elaborately built gates in masonry, of which the remains of the north, south and south-east gates can be seen. The remains of the brick piers which carried the gate structure are visible at the south-east gate, and the foundations of the flint and brick-faced north and south gates can be seen to the rear of the inturns of the later stone wall. The position of the west and east gates, with their double-carriageways, can be identified although their structural remains are not visible above the ground. The rampart itself survives as a grassy bank immediately inside the stone wall.

Although Calleva's rampart, like

Cross-section of the late second century town defences

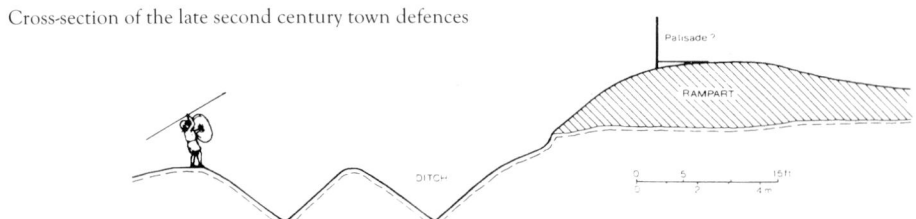

THE DEFENCES

those of other towns, is difficult to date closely, it is likely that its construction was occasioned either by the decision of the governor of Britain, Clodius Albinus, to take an army to fight with Septimius Severus for control of the empire in 196-7, or by the consequences of the damaging rebellion of the northern tribe of the Maeatae of 180-4.

Although the work was carried out fairly rapidly the defences seem to have enclosed all that was practicable to defend. This probably accounts for their rough 'diamond' shape. The same course was followed when the stone wall was constructed as a replacement in the years around 260-80.

South-east gate from within the town, 1976; brick piers encase the timber supports of the early gate, with the later town wall abutting on either side.

South gate from within the town, 1975; foundations of the gate building in the foreground. In the background is the later town wall

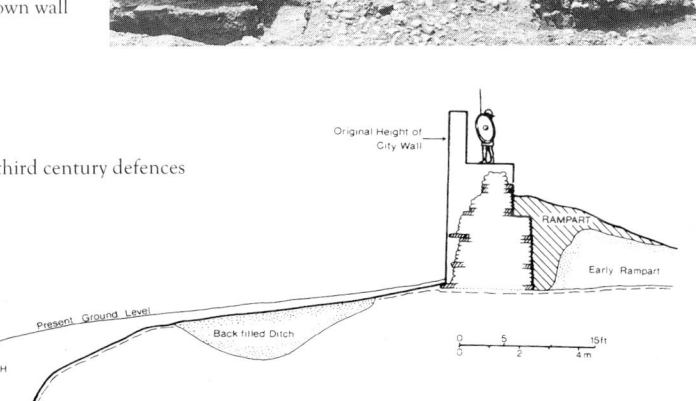

Cross-section of the late third century defences and city wall

THE DEFENCES

Not just in Britain, but all around the western empire, cities were providing themselves with strong defences in the face of the mounting unrest on the frontiers. The complete circuit of the wall (1½ miles; over 2.5km) survives above ground and, at its highest, now stands about 4.5m high by the south gate. Three metres thick at the base, it is built of flint quarried from the chalk and brought a distance of at least 6 ½ miles (10km). Every four to five courses of flint there is a bonding course of generally flattish slabs of stone. These consist of a variety of materials including limestone brought from as far afield as the Bath region about 50 miles (70-80 km). It has been estimated that at least 105,000 wagon loads of flint and 45,000 loads of bonding stones were required. Given the other requirements of materials and labour the whole undertaking would have consumed a huge part of the resource of the civitas of the Atrebates over several years. Although the wall has lost almost all traces of its outer surface, it remains an impressive monument. The southern section, with the south gate, particularly deserves a visit. The wall was originally fronted by a broad ditch about 14m wide of which a particularly good section is preserved in the copse around the south-western part of the wall.

Within the walls the plans are known of many buildings from aerial photography and excavations. None, however, is visible above ground.

The late third century town wall

South Gate in course of excavation 1975

16

(left and below)
Coins of Caratacus (left)
and Epatticus (right)

Late Roman gold finger-ring: the blue onyx is engraved with a satyr reaching down to a cupid

Late second century onyx cameo engraved with a bust of a young woman whose hairstyle is based on that of Faustina II, wife of the emperor Marcus Aurelius

The 'Church' at Silchester with the Forum and Basilica in the background

Gladiators fighting in the arena of the Calleva amphitheatre

Imaginative reconstruction of the South Gate of Calleva Atrebatum

Excavation of the North Gate during 1991

Aerial view of Silchester from the west: the Roman street plan, and the course of the town wall show clearly

Excavation in progress in Insula IX during 1999

THE FORUM BASILICA

The forum and adjoining basilica, situated in the middle of the town combined the functions of market place and seat of administration and justice both for the town and the civitas of the Atrebates. Altogether the building covered about 0.8 hectares (2 acres).

The forum was an open square lined by porticoes, shops and offices on three sides. The main entrance was designed in an elaborate fashion with a dedicatory inscription whose letters were 28cm high. On the fourth side stood the basilica, consisting of a great hall

Roman bronze eagle from the basilica

Plan of the Forum-basilica built in stone in about the mid-second century

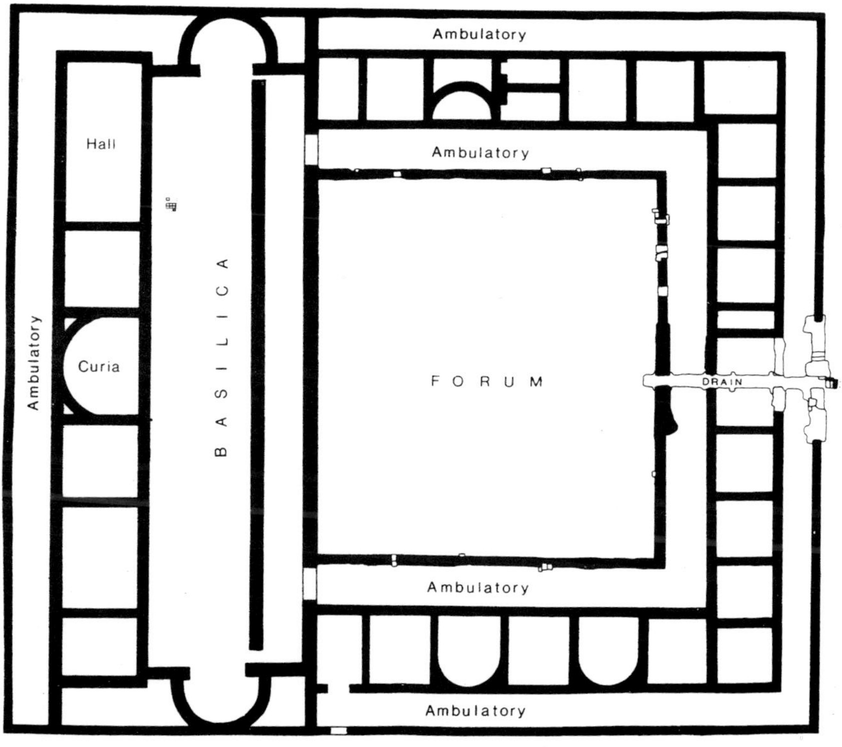

THE FORUM BASILICA

(about 82 by 17.5m), whose superstructure was carried on one row of Corinthian columns about 8.6m high. At either end were raised rooms, originally apsidal in plan, from which we might imagine the magistrates dispensing justice. On the west side was a suite of rooms or offices in the centre of which was an apsidal, marble-lined council chamber or shrine.

Recent excavation has clearly shown that this imposing new building was constructed towards the middle of the second century AD to replace the timber basilica and forum of comparable size and plan which had been erected in the late first century AD. Absence of traces of flooring in the basilica raises the possibility that the building was never finished.

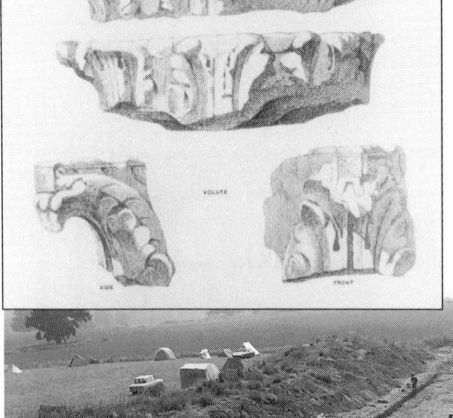

Fragments of Corinthian capitals from the basilica

Basilica in the course of excavation in 1981

THE FORUM BASILICA

A surprising discovery, made during the excavation of the masonry basilica was evidence for metalworking in the building from the mid-third century until the end of the Roman period. Iron-smithing seems to have been the most important occupation, but there were also residues from bronze-working. The presence of these activities makes it unlikely that the basilica continued to serve any administrative or judicial function during the later Roman period unless these functions were con- fined to the first floor, or the forum. It is unclear where such activities might otherwise have been carried out within the town.

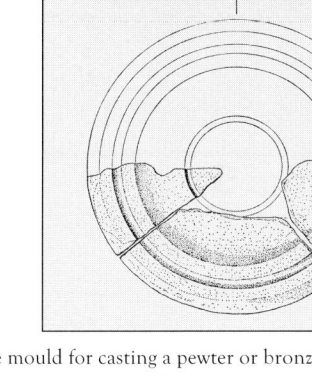

Limestone mould for casting a pewter or bronze dish (above)

(left) Half a mould from the basilica for producing copies of the coinage of the Gallic usurper Tetricus (A.D. 271-73). The cast shows a standing figure which represents SPES (hope)

Aerial view of the forum-basilica from the north

THE CHURCH

Close to the south-east corner of the forum is a small building only 13 by 9m consisting of a nave flanked by aisles, an apse to the west and a porch to the east. An important feature of the building is the transept, which serves to distinguish it from earlier, simple basilica-style structures. Within the apse was found a geometric mosaic of black and white chequers, of which the central motif is an equal-armed cross. Just 3.5m to the east of the porch is a tiled area, 1.2m square, which has been interpreted as the setting for a baptismal font. If the building is a church, it can hardly be earlier than 313, the year in which Christianity was first officially tolerated by Constantine the Great, but it has many features which are also found in pagan temples and, on a strict interpretation of the evidence, the building *could* be earlier than this, and therefore not Christian.

Lead sealing from basilica with Christogram (Chi-Rho)

Mosaic from the apse of the church

Reconstruction of the church with the corner of the forum in the background

Church in course of excavation in 1961

TEMPLES

There are no known temples of classical type at Calleva; instead native architectural traditions persisted. A typical example of a Romano-Celtic temple consists of a small central square shrine (the fanum) surrounded by an enclosed ambulatory; an unusual type is the polygonal building in Insula VII. Celtic Mars may perhaps be represented by some sculptured fragments in Insula XXXV and it is likely that Celtic deities, perhaps twinned with their Roman counterparts, rather than purely Roman gods, were worshipped in these temples. Foreign cults introduced to the citizens of Calleva included Sarapis, an Egyptian deity and, possibly, Mithras in Insula XIX.

Head of Egyptian god Sarapis

Reconstruction of Romano-Celtic temple (see below)

Excavated foundations of the Romano-Celtic temple in Insula XXXV in 1907

THE PUBLIC BATHS

South-east of the forum, on the side of the shallow valley along which runs a stream, stood the town baths. These were constructed in the first century AD, perhaps as early as the 50s, and were probably among the first Roman buildings constructed in the town. Originally they consisted of a portico with entrance from the street, an exercise yard (palaestra), an undressing room (apodyterium), a cold room with plunge-bath (frigidarium), a warm room (tepidarium), a hot room (caldarium) and a hot, dry bath (laconicum or sudatorium). The whole building measured 43.5 by 23m and was almost certainly supplied with water from the nearby stream as no evidence of any other source of water for it has been discovered.

Bathing in the ancient world was an elaborate affair: to clean the body it might first be smeared in oil, then exercise induced sweating and the dirt was scraped off the skin in the hot room with an instrument called a strigil. A dip in the cold plunge closed the pores and so concluded the ritual.

The baths underwent many periods of alteration and may eventually have offered facilities for both sexes. Otherwise men and women would have bathed at different times each day. The warm and hot rooms were heated by means of hypocausts where the floor was supported on short pillars (pilae) enabling hot air to circulate from a furnace attached to the outside of the room. Gases were carried upwards by flues made of box-tiles set in the walls to ceiling height. In order to provide adequate heating, each hot room had to be served by its own furnace.

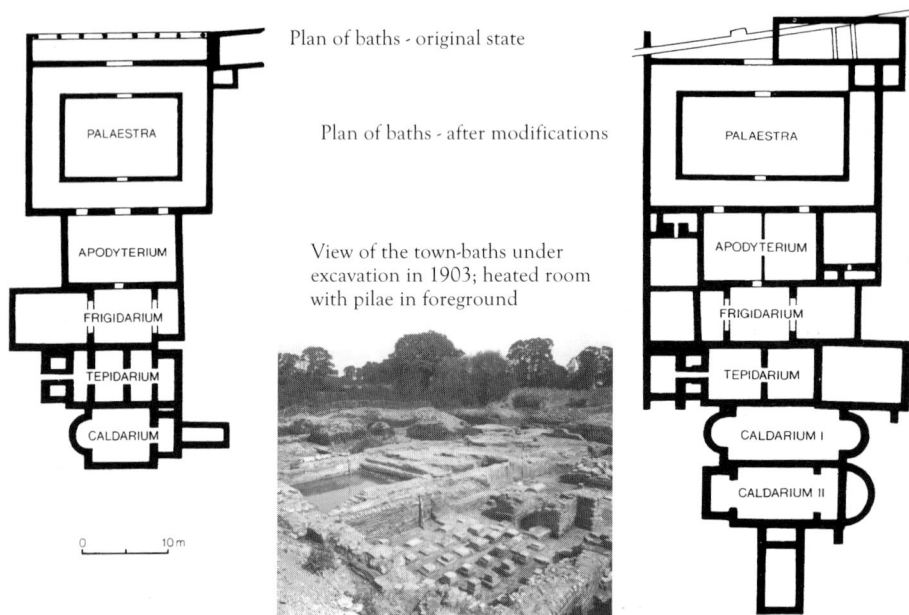

Plan of baths - original state

Plan of baths - after modifications

View of the town-baths under excavation in 1903; heated room with pilae in foreground

THE MANSIO

Towards the south gate in Insula VII is the second largest building of Roman Calleva. It has been identified as a mansio, or inn, which was specifically for the use of those using the imperial post, for rest and refreshment of personnel and mounts. It consists of three wings set around a large courtyard; each wing contains a suite of rooms of very similar dimensions, but the heated rooms are confined to the west wing. In the case of the north and south wings, the room arrangement is suggestive of self-contained suites grouped either side of small divided rooms. Similar symmetry may be detected in the west wing. Instead of an east wing there is an outer court to which is attached a bath-building in the south-east quarter. The duplication of rooms suggests that there was provision for bathing for both sexes. A latrine seems to have been a later addition on the southern side. Given the purpose of the building it is not surprising to find other examples, very similar in plan, in Britain and elsewhere. The nearest example to Calleva is that identified from aerial photographs at Wanborough in Wiltshire, about 30 miles (56 km) west of the town.

Plan of the inn (mansio) near the south gate

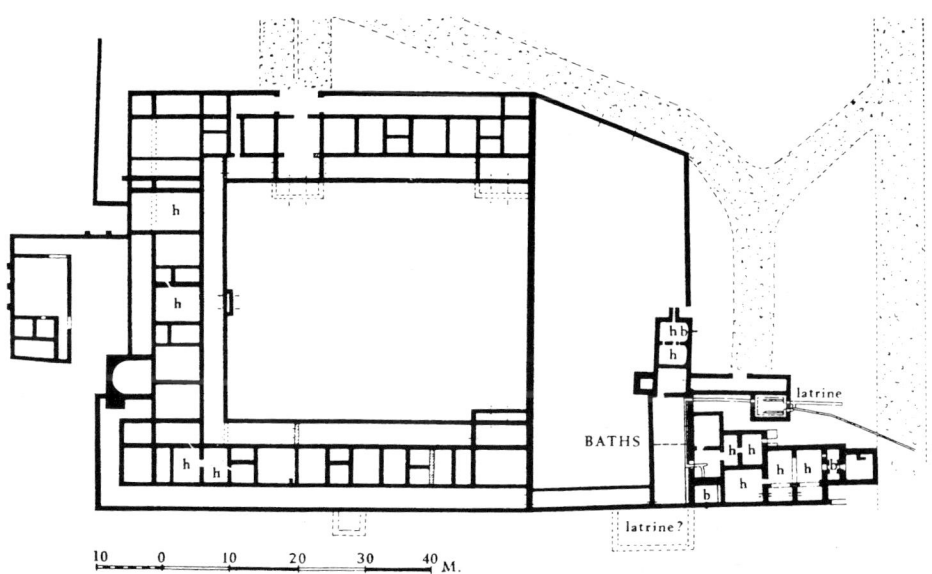

DOMESTIC HOUSING

There is a considerable range in the size and ground-plan of private houses within the walls of Calleva, with the earliest examples in masonry dating back to the late first century AD. There are small rectangular buildings without any internal sub-divisions, but with evidence of a hearth or furnace which could have served as houses, workshops, or a combination of both. Larger, single-range houses occur with internal sub-divisions and then either one or two corridors alongside to give privacy to individual rooms. The provision of projecting wing rooms marks the next elaboration in ground plan, and this is followed by houses where additional wings were added. Although never designed like this from the start, house 1 in Insula XIV eventually grew to have four wings enclosing a courtyard. Such a grand development, perhaps slowly evolving over several generations, was exceptional; most houses having no more than one range, perhaps with projecting wing-rooms.

Fine tableware pottery vessels, first and second century (left)

Mosaic pavement from house in Insula XIV (below)

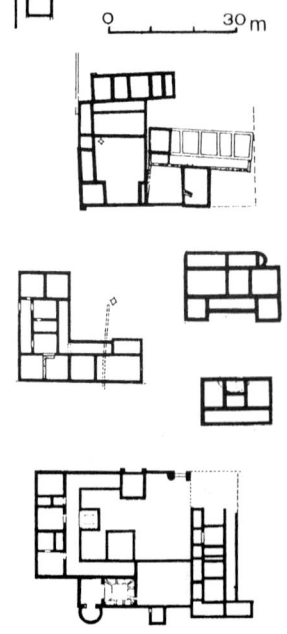

A range of shop and house plans

DOMESTIC HOUSING

All these houses were provided with masonry foundations which, in many cases, supported an upper storey. The principal rooms can be identified by the presence of mosaics, tiled or tessellated floors and under-floor heating. The majority of rooms had plain floors of cement or gravel and some of these may have had raised, plank floors. Heated rooms are reasonably common, but only one private house seems to have been provided with a bath-house. Roofing was of ceramic tiles or thatch, with stone 'slates' of limestone or sandstone becoming more common in the later Roman period. Window glass is a relatively common find suggesting that many windows were glazed.

Interior decoration was limited to painted wall plaster and, more rarely, the provision of mosaics, evidence of which has been found in some thirty houses. Most of the wall plaster was too fragmentary to reconstruct but one section has been reconstructed with a flower pattern. The majority of mosaics so far discovered are of geometric designs, with only a few examples of figured subjects. Using stone of mostly southern British origin, colours are predominantly red, yellow and grey, outlined in black against a white background. While some surviving examples date back to at least the second century, the majority belong to the third and fourth centuries.

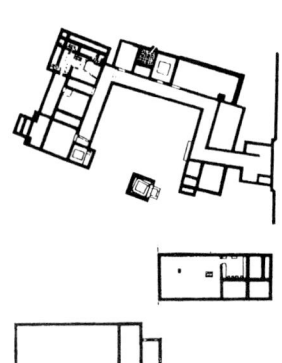

(left) House plans, with that of house 1, insula XIV at the bottom

Mosaic head of Ceres

Reconstruction of a Roman living room (below)

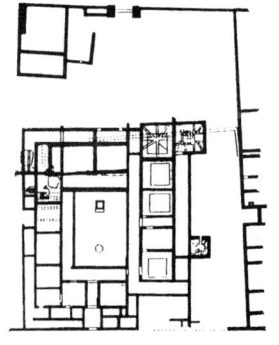

WATER SUPPLY AND DRAINAGE

Water is to be found in abundance beneath the shallow gravel-capping of the Silchester spur. From the late Iron Age onwards it was mostly obtained by means of wells dug to a depth no greater than 6m, and often no deeper than 3m. The shafts were generally lined with wood to prevent collapse and the remains of both purpose-built 'box' linings and discarded wine-barrels specifically reused for this purpose have been found. Water was presumably raised in buckets, but there is one example of a wooden force-pump with leaden cylinders which could have delivered about three gallons a minute.

There is no certain evidence of an aqueduct supply to Silchester and this is not surprising given the height of the settlement in relation to the surrounding land. The nearest higher ground with springs and streams that could be tapped is the north Hampshire chalk at least six miles (10 km) distant. However, the existence of one deeply lined wooden water-pipe which ran along the southern margin of Insulae XV and XVI and deep beneath the defences is evidence that some water was brought from outside the settlement. The actual source of water for the pipe is unknown but, if the nearest stream was tapped, the water would have to have been raised to the level of the pipe. A puzzle also surrounds the water supply to the town baths. The latrine suggests the nearby stream might have been exploited, but close by there are also remains of wooden piling, perhaps to carry wooden troughs from a source of water in Insula VI or XXXV.

Apart from their latrines which emptied into a wood-lined cess-pit, the town baths exploited the small adjacent stream to drain waste water while the baths attached to the mansio were drained via a wooden channel through the south-east gate. Otherwise there was no organised drainage scheme to dispose of sewage and waste water from Calleva. To be effective drainage systems depended upon a continuous supply of running water and that, as we have seen, was not available to the citizens of the town. Refuse and night-soil was either disposed of in pits in back yards or taken out by cart from the town.

Imported wine barrels re-used as well-linings

Wooden force-pump with leaden cylinders

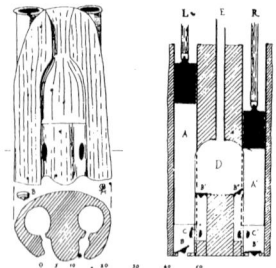

SUBURBS AND CEMETERIES

Apart from the exploration of the amphitheatre there has been no lengthy investigation of the Roman suburbs by excavation. Most of what we know is derived from a study of aerial photographs and the systematic collection of building debris, pottery and other artefacts from the surface of ploughed fields. Such investigation has revealed that the suburbs extended at least half a mile beyond the east and west gates, but rather less to the south. At the back of the small rectangular buildings ranged along the Cirencester road are small allotments and paddocks.

Except for the occasional cremation revealed by the plough and the discovery of one inscribed tombstone in 1577, the cemeteries remain unknown, but their location appears to lie beyond the 'Outer Earthwork' to the north and west. Thus the former population of Calleva remains, virtually undisturbed, for future generations to research.

Beyond the cemeteries and suburbs lay fairly open country with only a little woodland, as the study of the ancient pollen has begun to show. The land seems to have been given over to pasture rather than the cultivation of cereals. West of the town, the plateau gravels seem to have supported a similar heathland vegetation to that which grows there today.

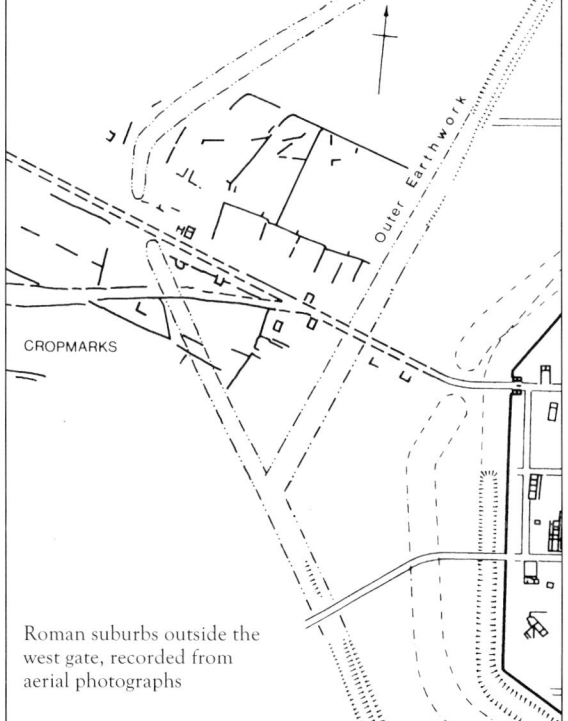

Roman suburbs outside the west gate, recorded from aerial photographs

Tombstone inscribed in Latin.
A translation reads:
'To the memory of Flavia Victorina Titus Tammonius',
Her husband set this up

THE END OF CALLEVA

The course of the town's decline and eventual abandonment is difficult to trace because the early excavators were not skilled enough to recognise that process, nor the traces of the more ephemeral buildings that might have succeeded the solid masonry houses as they came to be deserted. However, the current excavation in insula IX, close to the heart of the town, has shown no evidence of abandonment before the fifth century. This chimes with the work that has been carried out at other towns in Britain which gives us a frame-work for understanding what might have

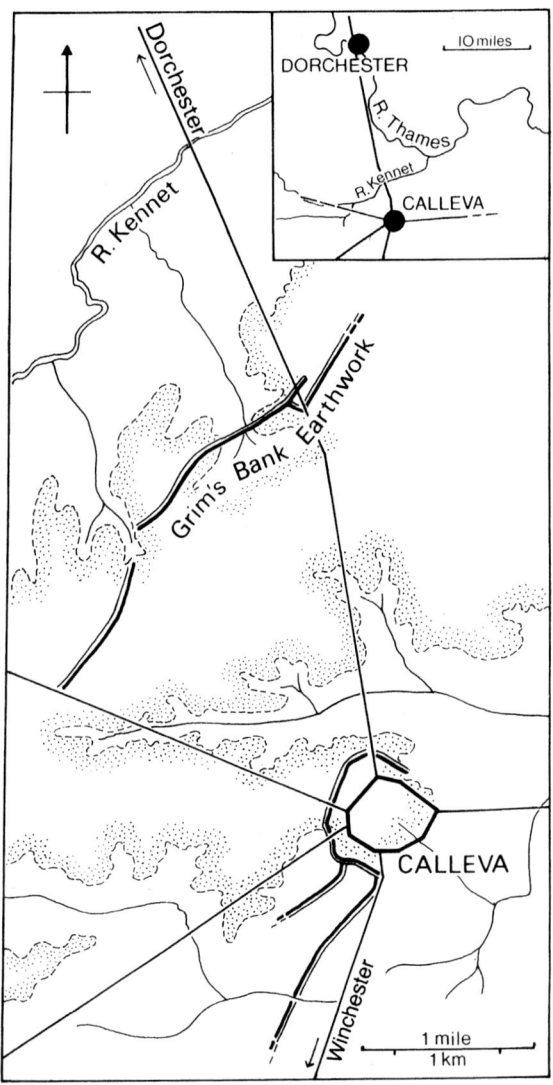

Silchester: late Roman earthworks outside the town

A Roman column reused as a property marker in the fifth century and found within the town. The stone is inscribed in Ogham script whose characters consist of horizontal lines scored in relation to a vertical axis, substituting for letters of the latin alphabet. The language is Celtic. An otherwise unknown man called Tebicatus is commemorated.

THE END OF CALLEVA

happened at Silchester. It shows that urban life throughout the island declined rapidly after 400. Even if some community survived the fifth century as the forerunner of the medieval village, Calleva cannot be regarded as a town in a Roman sense much after the middle decades of the fifth century.

We can only speculate as to why early medieval Silchester never grew to be a town as was the case with other Roman towns. One important reason will have been the emergence of the Anglo-Saxon kingdom of Wessex. The influence of early Saxon settlement around the former small town of Dorchester-upon-Thames was such that by AD 635 the town had become the centre of a bishopric. The dwindling Romano-British population of Silchester may have been responsible for defending a small enclave around the town, as evidenced, perhaps, by the earthworks which block the Roman road to Dorchester about two miles north of Calleva. By the later seventh century Winchester, only 23 miles to the south, had emerged as the principal centre of Wessex. Through evidence for the deliberate infilling of wells, the current excavations in insula IX hint at the possibility that the end of occupation was precipitated by a deliberate abandonment.

Although Silchester is mentioned in Domesday book, the earliest physical evidence that we have of the medieval village is the parish church of St Mary, whose visible fabric dates from about the mid-twelfth century, and occupation of similar date from the amphitheatre. The arena has produced evidence of a hall building, while the crest of the seating bank, which forms an ideal basis for a defensive work, and the southern entrance provide evidence for limited fortification as a temporary stronghold. This invites identification with the Castellum de Silva (whose location is not otherwise known) which, according to a chronicle of his reign, was taken by King Stephen in 1147 during his war against Matilda.

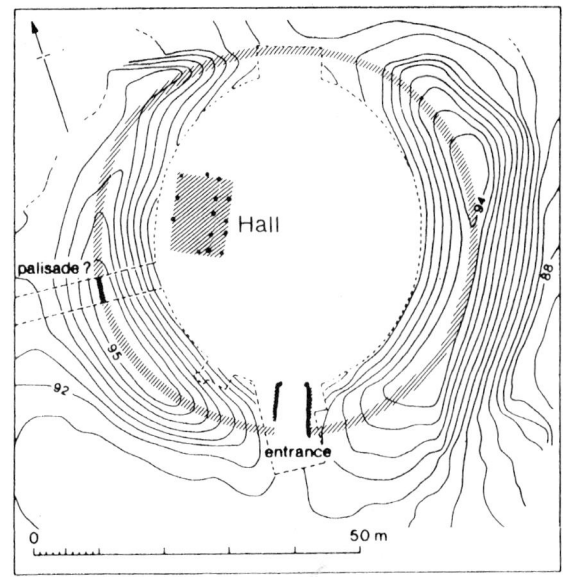

Amphitheatre in the mid twelfth century

HISTORY OF THE EXCAVATIONS

Our knowledge of Roman Silchester is founded on the extensive excavations carried out within the town walls during the second half of the nineteenth and the beginning of the twentieth century. The most notable investigation was that by the Society of Antiquaries of London between 1890 and 1909 which had the aim of revealing the whole life and history of a Roman town. The techniques of the time were sufficient to recover the plans of buildings with stone foundations but were inadequate for tackling many fundamental problems such as the chronology of the settlement, its Iron Age origins and its early Roman development.

Subsequent work in other towns of Roman Britain made it clear that timber predominated in the first and

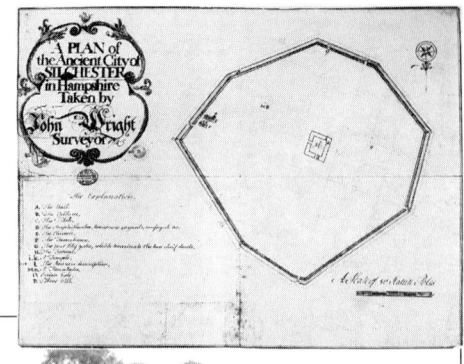

Plan of Silchester, 1745

Directors of the Silchester Excavation Fund in 1900

HISTORY OF THE EXCAVATIONS

second centuries AD, and wooden buildings appear also to be a feature of Roman towns in their later years. Since evidence of timber buildings was not recovered by the early excavations, the plan we do have is very much that of the town in the third and fourth centuries AD when the town was defended and stone building had become common.

Little new excavation was undertaken after 1909 because it was believed that the early work had been comprehensive. However, since the 1970s the University of Reading has become increasingly involved in new excavations directed by Professor Michael Fulford. Following work on the amphitheatre and forum basilica, which revealed remarkably good preservation of Iron Age and early Roman occupation, a project is currently under way exploring one of the central *insulae* of the town. It is abundantly clear that the scope for further work inside and outside the walls is enormous.

Some of the excavation team in 2000

Some of the locals who worked on the excavations of 1890-1909

VISITING THE SITE

Park in the public car park in Wall Lane from where you can walk the entire circuit of the well preserved Roman town walls, passing the sites of the North, South and South-East Gates, and crossing the lane to visit the amphitheatre. Normally, during July and August, on weekdays and weekends you will find the excavations in progress. They are accessible from the droveway (public bridle-way) which crosses the town. No visit would be complete without seeing the medieval parish church of St Mary's on the eastern side of the town.

If you have time for a longer visit, a walk to Rampier Copse, to the south-west of the Roman walled town, to see the well preserved Iron Age rampart is highly recommended. The rampart stands almost 5 metres above the bottom of the ditch. The footpath is signed to the left, just after you have passed through the line of the Roman walls and the site of the West Gate, as you head west along the Drove towards the modern village.

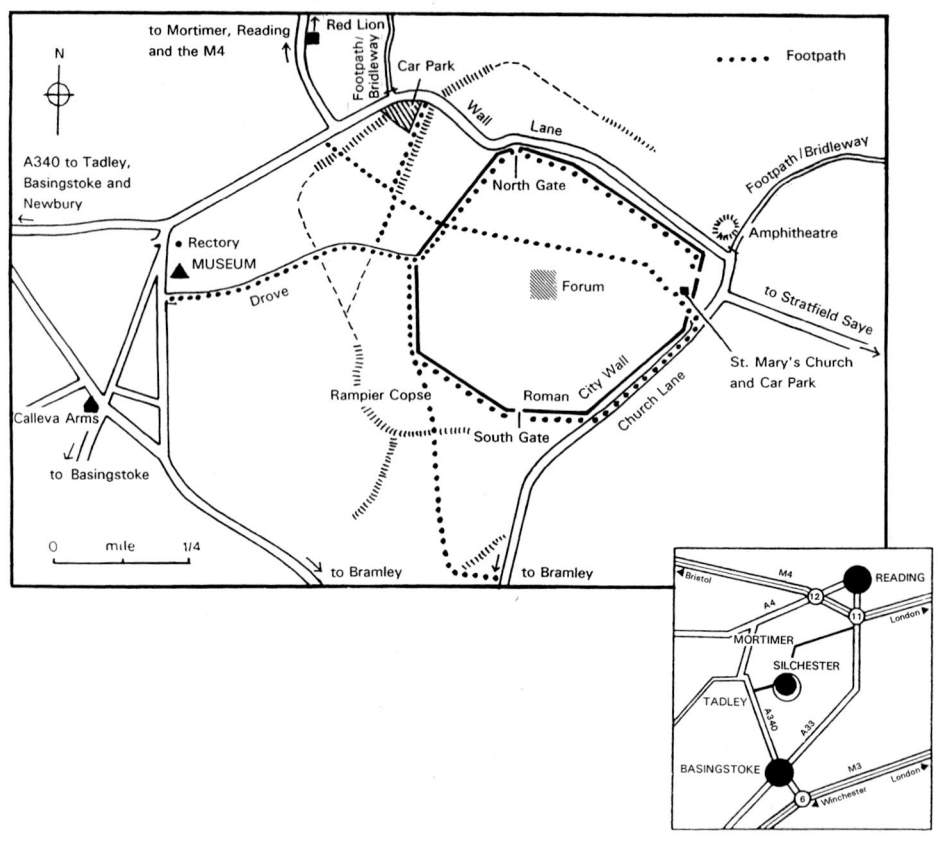